THE PSR KID

Aisha Rehema-Gist Henderson

Illustrations: Jennifer Rose O'Shay

A Division of Manifold Grace Publishing House

The PSR Kid
Copyright © 2021 Aisha Rehema-Gist Henderson

Cover design: Jennifer Rose O'Shay
Illustrations: Jennifer Rose O'Shay
Photog: Sarae Daniels
Editor: Precios Armstrong

ISBN: 978-1-952926-16-7

Printed in the United States of America

Published by PeeWee Press, a Division of Manifold Grace Publishing House, LLC
Southfield, Michigan 48033
www.manifoldgracepublishinghouse.com

Dedication

The PSR Kid is dedicated to all of the students I have worked with in the past, and presently, during my time as a School Social Worker (SSW). Their stories, and their fight to excel in the classroom, are the reasons I wanted to develop the PSR technique. It is my belief that by presenting this technique to my students, they will learn emotional control and focus on what they can control in their environment. I have observed that students who have utilized the PSR technique have been able to regulate their emotions; stay in the classroom more; and take breaks when needed. As I continue to observe my students progress, and sometimes regression, it has motivated me to share the PSR technique with other parents, caregivers, and professionals. I am excited to see how the PSR technique can help other students, schools, and families.

ACKNOWLEDGMENTS

I would like to acknowledge the following people who contributed to making *The PSR Kid* possible. This includes thanking a special man who was essential in making *The PBIS Song* a reality, as well as a true inspiration to the story line presented.

I also want to thank my poetry mentor. She was essential in guiding me through the publishing process and giving me the connections needed to make *The PSR Kid*.

Lastly, I want to thank God for giving me the strength to complete this project, my mother for blessing me with my writing and editorial skills; and my illustrator who brought the main character, Casper, to life. My illustrator did an amazing job and was a true asset to the team.

BACKGROUND

PSR is an acronym for Positive Self-Regulation. It is derived from the self-regulation theory that was created by Alberta Bandura. Alberta Bandura saw self-regulation as a tool to assist individuals with controlling their impulses, and to think through a situation before reacting to it. This same theory can be used in the classroom to help students learn how to manage their emotions in a positive way.

For example, the PSR is a technique that students have come to utilize in the classroom to identify and understand their emotions; monitor their body temperature; and identify a coping skill they can use in the moment. This technique is not yet evidence based; however, it has proven to be an effective tool in the classroom, in conjunction with the PBIS (Positive Behavior Interventions and Supports) model and "The PBIS song."

By using the PSR technique in combination with the PBIS model and "The PBIS song," students have learned to be safe, respectful, and responsible. They are now taking the time to stop, think, and regulate their emotions. As a School Social Worker (SSW), I have helped teachers, support staff, and the intervention team promote the PSR technique, in and out of the classroom. This has allowed students to focus more on what's in their control and how they can problem-solve without being aggressive toward staff and their peers. They have also learned how to resolve conflict in a positive manner.

To help your students learn more about the PSR technique there are resources following the story.

Introduction

Casper Mineo is a 12-year-old African American male who lives in Chicago, Illinois with his mother. His father has been incarcerated for the last 7 years. Casper has been having issues at school with controlling his temper, as well as, not responding to his classmate's negative comments. In the past, Casper believed that the only way to solve his problems at school were through verbal and/or physical aggression. He adopted this belief because he thought it would stop his classmates from making negative comments about his clothing and/or hygiene. However, Casper's constant aggression toward his peers only resulted in him being removed from the classroom and his grades to suffer.

Casper's mother, Dorothy, had become extremely exhausted from Casper's behavior at school and is tired of the constant phone calls. So, to get Casper under control, Dorothy decided to transfer Casper to Chadway Middle School. This is an alternative school in the Chicago area.

Dorothy heard that Chadway is a school for diverse learners and has helped students improve in attendance, academics and behaviors. She has also heard that Chadway uses a new method called the PSR technique. It has been used to reduce student's aggressive behaviors and provide them with the tools needed to stay in the classroom. Of course, Chadway Middle School was not Casper's first choice However, as time went on, Casper was able to gain a sense of accomplishment and acceptance as he attended Chadway Middle School. Most of his acceptance toward his new school came from meeting his new friend, Johnny Lion, and the School Counselor, Ms. Wilson.

Throughout this book, we will see whether or not Johnny Lion and Ms. Wilson can help Casper stay in the classroom and learn emotional control. Join us as we learn more about Casper's middle school experience, and if the PSR technique has helped him thrive in his new school environment.

PSR kids know how to stop, think and regulate their emotions. They also know the benefits of staying in the classroom without worrying about getting into trouble or getting behind in their schoolwork.

PSR kids are not influenced by their peers' negative comments or actions. They have learned to focus on what is in their control to make better choices within their environment.

So, now that we know what a PSR kid is, let's learn about a PSR kid named Casper Mineo, and his journey to changing his behavior.

Casper Mineo is a 12-year-old African American male, who attends Natural View Middle School in Chicago. He has been attending this school since the sixth grade. During Casper's time at Natural View he has had issues trying to improve his grades and his behavior. Most of Casper's teachers and peers assumed he would change his behavior once he entered the 7th grade. However, Casper's behavior actually got worse. Now he is getting into daily arguments and physical altercations with his peers. He is known to his peers and the staff as the "highly emotional kid." They resorted to giving Casper this label because he was constantly enraged. To Casper, if people are going to categorize him, there's no need for him to attend class, especially if he feels targeted or messed with. "It's a waste of time," he thought.

Casper was adamant about not attending class and hated the idea of staying there. He knew that by entering any classroom his peers would taunt him about his appearance or make violent gestures (e.g. getting in his face threatening to harm him, etc.). although Casper had some desire to stay in the classroom and behave, he found it hard to ignore his classmates. He often feared that if he didn't respond to his classmates, they would think of him as weak. Casper didn't want to deal with that either.

So, Casper continued to react to his peers' comments. Most of his reactions were in the form of an argument. For example, Casper would argue with his classmates when they called him "Stupid" or "Ugly!" He would also argue with them when they made statements like, "You're wearing your sister's clothes! Why do you stink so bad?" These comments made Casper so angry. He would often ball up his fists, to show his classmates that he would fight anyone who poked at him.

Since Casper didn't come from money, he felt that he always had to defend himself. It didn't matter if his classmates were talking about his clothes or his hygiene. He just knew he had to respond to them in order to avoid looking weak. But, after a while, Casper realized that arguing with his peers only made the situation worse. It didn't actually stop his classmates from making jokes or bullying him. It only gave them more ammunition to say something else and someone from his class always had something to say.

With all of the drama at school, Casper was not doing well in his classes. His teachers accused him of having no self-control; no sense of focus; and not completing his work. They would also kick him out of class if he refused to stop arguing with another student. Over time, it became obvious to Casper's teachers that he didn't care about his education. His report card was a mere reflection of that; especially since he was failing all of his classes except for gym. However, Casper's mom, Dorothy, was fed up with his behavior and did not find his grades acceptable.

Dorothy was tired of Casper failing his classes! She was also tired of going to Casper's school constantly, because he couldn't control his temper or get along with his classmates. Dorothy had enough. She stated, "I work two jobs! I can't afford to be picking up Casper from his school every other day, just because he wants to misbehave. Casper's got to get it together!"

Dorothy believed that the first step to modifying Casper's behavior was changing his school environment and enrolling him in an alternative school. The alternative school that Dorothy chose was Chadway Middle School. Chadway Middle School is an alternative school, in Chicago, that caters to student's diverse learning styles. It is also known for promoting the PSR (positive self-regulation) technique.

The PSR technique is a teaching tool that students use to regulate their emotions, and interact with their peers in a positive way.

Dorothy believed that by Casper attending Chadway Middle School he would be able to thrive in his classes, and receive additional tools to fit his learning style.

However, Casper still wasn't thrilled about attending Chadway. He thought, "Chadway would be just like my other school. I'll be forced to defend myself, again, against other student's who tease me, or bully me. I know my mom wants me to think that things will be different here. But, I just can't imagine anything changing. Kids are going to be mean no matter what. This school is not going to stop that from happening, or me having a temper."

Yet, Casper began to change his mind, slightly, after meeting the PSR kid, Johnny Lion. Johnny Lion told Casper, "Man, my behavior was just like yours before I came to Chadway. I had no idea how to control my emotions. I just knew I had a lot of emotions inside, and didn't care how they came out. But thankfully, Chadway showed me how to express my feelings and saved me from making bad choices. So, bro, I get it!"

Johnny continued to tell Casper, "It's not easy to control your emotions after you have told your classmate, repeatedly, to stop trash talking you. It's even harder to let the idea of fighting go, especially when you think hitting the person would solve everything. But being at Chadway, I realized that my responses matter. I also enjoy making my own decisions too much to let one comment throw me off my square. I know this sounds weak. But bruh, I have to keep it 100! I also want you to know that it's possible to control your temper and stay out of trouble."

Casper felt Johnny had mad wisdom. However, he wasn't convinced that a non-violent approach (e.g. not responding or fighting his peers) would resolve anything. He believed that the situation would only get worse, and his peers would see him as an easy target. "Open season for bullying!" according to him.

With Casper's concerns, he still continued to ponder over Johnny's non-violent approach. He asked himself, "What would it be like to ignore my classmate's negative comments? Would this mean that I wouldn't argue with them anymore; or, have any physical aggression? Would I seem weak to them?"

Casper couldn't imagine being less aggressive. But a part of him felt that it may be possible. And, he thought, "What other ways could I solve my problems? Do these options even exist or work? Could these new ways of doing things actually change me? Who would I be if I wasn't angry? To be honest, I'm not even sure what I'm actually angry about!"

Casper thought about the things that triggered him, as well as made him angry. He realized that his past experiences still haunted him.

Specifically, Casper was 5 years old when his father went to prison for life. It was the worst day of his life. He never thought in a million years that his father would be taken away by the cops or he would see their memories slowly fade. Unfortunately, there was nothing Casper could do. He remembers that day vividly. As Casper watched his dad be taken by the cops, he felt all their memories slowly fading. He had no idea if he would see his father ever again.

For Casper, it was hard not thinking about all of the memories they shared together, such as playing sports, dancing in the living room, and rapping to their favorite artists or songs. Casper loved his dad. But now that Casper's dad was in prison, he felt ashamed and angry at him. He was also embarrassed about sharing this information with anyone. Especially since he couldn't understand why his father was taken away and had to leave their family.

So, Casper continued to reflect on his anger. During his reflection, he thought about his mom and their relationship. Even though things weren't bad between them, he noticed that their relationship had changed.

In the past, Casper and his mom would dance and sing around the kitchen while they baked. It was their thing to do. But, now that his dad was in prison, his mom had to work more and carry the household work alone. This meant Casper had less time with his mom, and was unable to get the flyest gear. To Casper, having the flyest gear was something he wanted because he was tired of being teased at school. He also missed his mom a great deal, which sometimes led to him keeping his feelings to himself for fear of being a burden.

To top it off, Casper was diagnosed with ADHD at the age of six. With everything else going on, Casper couldn't stand feeling different because of his ADHD. He hated the fact that he would be hyper at times or had a difficult time focusing in class.

Of course, Casper tried to forget about all of the changes that were happening at school, and at home. But it was too hard to ignore. He continued to think about his dad's incarceration and how his mom was forced to work more. Again, he didn't like having ADHD; but he knew it was a part of his daily life. After reflecting on everything, Casper realized he had a lot of weight on his shoulders, and needed to talk things out. So, he decided to take a chance and talk to Johnny about everything.

Casper told Johnny everything.

Johnny reacted, "Bruh! That's a lot to deal with. No wonder it's been hard for you to stay in class. I couldn't imagine being in your shoes. But, I appreciate you sharing your story though. That was really cool of you. And just to be honest, my dad is also locked up. And it's been hard on my family too. But, what has helped me with my frustration, stress, and anger, was me sharing my story with a trusted friend, School Counselor, or School Social Worker."

Johnny continued the conversation with Casper, by telling him more about Chadway's School Counselor. Johnny stated, "The School Counselor at Chadway is dope! She gave me some really cool tools to manage my emotions in class. It has helped me to keep myself in check. At first, I was hesitant about changing my reaction to things. But after a while, her suggestions and tools seemed to work. I have been in more control of myself ever since. I even figured out what I was good at. You know, besides the norm, like basketball and football," he chuckled.

Casper shared his story with the School Counselor, Ms. Wilson. Ms. Wilson was open to hearing what Casper had to say, and was glad that he trusted her with his information.

I'm glad you listened to your friend Johnny, and stopped by. He definitely is a good role model here at Chadway."

Casper gave the School Counselor a blank stare after she mentioned the worksheet and felt his mind racing. He thought, "This Counselor is crazy! How are these strategies really going to help me? What does she even mean by regulating my emotions? This is insane!" However, Casper couldn't think of any other solutions. He knew he would have to, either work with the School Counselor, or deal with his mom's constant nagging. Casper refused to hear his mom's mouth anymore. He believed that the best thing to do was to give counseling a try. He said, "If Johnny can do it, so can I. He's a pretty cool guy for our age."

Casper completed the worksheet and reviewed it with Ms. Wilson.

Emotional Regulation Worksheet

Identify Your Triggers	Identify Body Cues	Identify Coping Skills
Name calling (e.g, ugly, stupid, dumb, etc.)	Head gets hot	Take deep breaths and count from 15 to 1 backwards.
Talking about my clothes	Tighten my fist	Using self-talk, remind yourself of the consequences.
Hygiene	Voice elevates	Tell the student to stop and ignore the comment by removing yourself from the situation with the teacher's permission.
Body stance or posture	Leg starts to shake	Take another seat in the room, ask to take a break in the hallway or sit in another quiet place in the school.
		Write out your feelings on paper, or in a journal.

As Casper and Ms. Wilson reviewed the worksheet, he told her how he usually responds to his classmates. Casper said, "Once I get triggered by a peer, my leg starts to shake. It doesn't matter if a peer calls me a name or talks about my clothes, my leg is going to move. Then, my mind goes blank; and, my body goes into fight mode. I am no longer in control of my emotions."

Ms. Wilson said, "Casper that makes sense. It's difficult not to respond, or fight someone if they make a negative comment towards you. However, it's still important for you to try to control your emotions, to avoid escalating the situation further. With that said, is there anything else in that moment that might push you over the edge? This could be a person staring at you or laughing at you; calling you names; or getting in your face to start a fight.

Casper said, "It could be all of those things Ms. Wilson. But the main thing that pushes me over the edge, is when a classmate gets the entire class to make fun of me. Once that happens, I feel stupid. All I want then, is for the class to stop laughing at me."

Ms. Wilson, with compassion said, "Casper, it sounds as if comments like that have really hurt your feelings. It can't be easy to turn a negative situation around when the rest of your class is laughing too. So, I can understand why you would want to resort to fighting."

Ms. Wilson continued to talk to Casper, and made a brief assessment of his emotional control in the classroom. She said, "Casper, from what you are explaining to me, the classroom environment seems to be overwhelming, and very confining for you. Almost like you're trapped in a maze and can't find your way out. If that is the case, I would recommend that you take a pause so that you're aware of your body cues, then, take a deep breath. Remember, when it comes to your brain, there are two parts that work together. These parts of the brain are your amygdala and your prefrontal cortex.

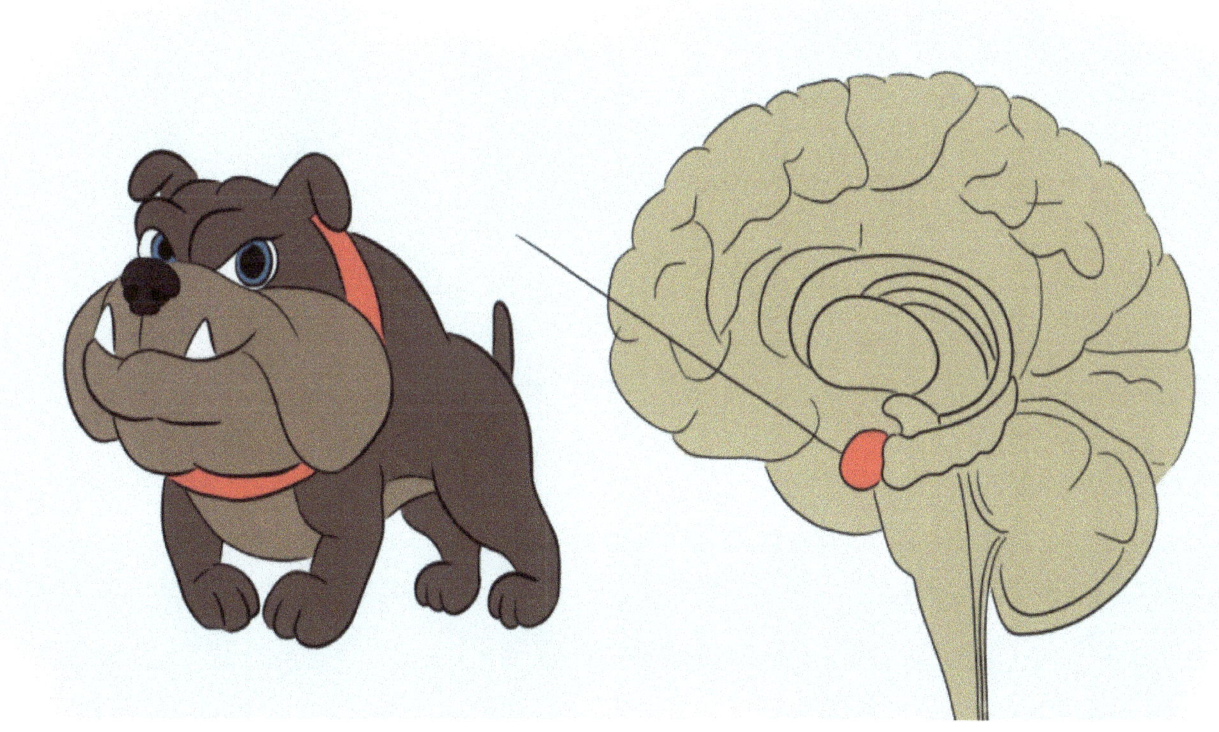

Your amygdala is the region of your brain that controls your emotions. It is considered your "Watch Dog." When your 'Watch Dog" activates, its goal is to protect you from harm or danger. It is also used to tell your body to go into fight or flight mode, or a freeze state."

Ms. Wilson went on to describe the prefrontal cortex. She explained, "The prefrontal cortex is the region of the brain that guides a person's decision making, and reminds them that there are consequences to their actions. The prefrontal cortex is also known as the "Wise OWL." The "Wise OWL's" job is to help the body stay calm; provide an individual with clear thoughts and impulse control; as well as problem-solve a situation without a person reacting to his or her first thought."

"So, Casper, in your case, when your classmates laugh at you or make negative comments, what do you need in that moment to stay calm?" asked Ms. Wilson.

"Honestly, Ms. Wilson, I think I need to check in with my body more. This way I can see how my body reacts when all of these things happen. For example, if my leg begins to shake, or I get a tickle in my throat, I need to decide what that means for my response. Specifically, would that mean I would yell at my classmates or punch them in the face? If yes, I need to decide, at that moment, how to stop that aggressive response. This might include me counting from ten; using positive self-talk; moving to another seat; or taking a break from the classroom. If I decide to take a break from the classroom, I know I would need to ask my teacher if I could (1) step into the hallway; (2) go to the main office or your office; or (3) call my mom for extra support. I never really tried these strategies before, but I think they could work. What do you think about that plan Ms Wilson?" Casper responded.

Ms. Wilson smiled, "Casper, I think the strategies you developed are an excellent idea! Just know, it can still be difficult in the beginning to control your emotions. However, if you practice checking in with your body at home, it'll get easier to control your emotions at school. So, try to practice these steps with your mom. Remember, grown-ups have a hard time regulating their emotions too. Practice is so important. Practice, practice, practice!"

Casper took Ms. Wilson's advice and practiced trying to stop and think before reacting to his peers. He found that by pausing, and checking in with himself, his leg would shake and his fists would tighten. These body movements would occur after his classmates made several comments about him. Once that happened, Casper knew it was time to count from ten to one, then take a deep breath. With all of the practice that Casper put in, he couldn't believe he was now in control of his emotions. It was like a miracle!

Casper was elated by all of the praises he was receiving at home and at school. He was also excited to tell Ms. Wilson how essential she was in helping him stay in the classroom. One day, Casper ran to Ms. Wilson's office and said, "Thank you, Ms. Wilson! Your methods were so helpful in the classroom. I plan to continue using these coping skills until they don't work anymore, and continue to stay aware of my body signals. This way I can keep my Watch Dog under control. If these coping skills stop working, we can always talk about it, right? And try something else?"

Ms. Wilson put her hand on Casper's shoulder and replied, "Absolutely, Casper! I am so proud of you! You have been able to stay in the classroom for an entire month now. That means you are officially a PSR Kid. I think it's time for you to learn "The PBIS song, Regulate Your Emotions". Let's call Johnny in, so he can celebrate with us!"

 "For sure Ms. Wilson," Casper replied proudly.

As Johnny entered the room, Ms. Wilson told the kids, "Let's get this song started!"

The PBIS SONG

Intro
PBIS Kid...
We're about to do the PBIS Dance...
So, let's get ready...

Put your hands on your thighs to show you are stopping. Then take your index finger and point at your head. This shows that you are thinking before takin' action. Now, bring your hands in front of you and move them around your belly so can control our breathing. Now, let's put it together.
Stop...think...and regulate your emotions...
Stop...think...and regulate your emotions...
Stop...think...and regulate your emotions...(3x)

Verse 1
Being a kid of class...commotion...
My body was out of control.
My feelings were madness.
I didn't know what to do.

Verse 2
My parents talking crazy,
Cuz they know I could do better.
My brain no longer caring.
So, my choices cost me my freedom.

Verse 3
My anthem offline
...With no peer connection
But when I became a PBIS kid...
My anthem became live cuz

Verse 4
PBIS kids are motionless, unstoppable, un-deni-ably intelligent
Managing their emotions before fists are pumpin', body pausing.
So, they can do their PBIS dance...

Chorus
Stop...think...and regulate your emotions...
Stop...think...and regulate your emotions...
Stop...think...and regulate your emotions...(3)

Verse 5
Now that I'm PBIS kid, I can control my emotions.
I can stay in the classroom with no problem.
Hater comments no longer my business.
Dog walking inexistent, PBIS kid in the building.
Doing my dance.

Chorus
Stop...think...and regulate your emotions...
Stop...think...and regulate your emotions...
Stop...think...and regulate your emotions...(3x)

This song was created as a supplemental tool to help implement PBIS in the school system. However, it does not represent, and is not affiliated with, the national center of PBIS. You can hear the PBIS song by going to this website: https://www.youtube.com/watch?v=8sWe9yyG8Ks

Additional Resources

The Emotional Regulation worksheet is used to help students understand their emotions, and to become self-aware. It can also help students with controlling their impulses as well as identify healthy coping skills. Each student can complete this worksheet to learn more about themselves and practice self-regulation.

Emotional Regulation Worksheet

Identify Your Triggers	Identify Body Cues	Identify Coping Skills

The Control Wheel is used to help students understand the things that are, or are not, in their control. This wheel can also help students with impulse control - reset themselves; and remain calm.

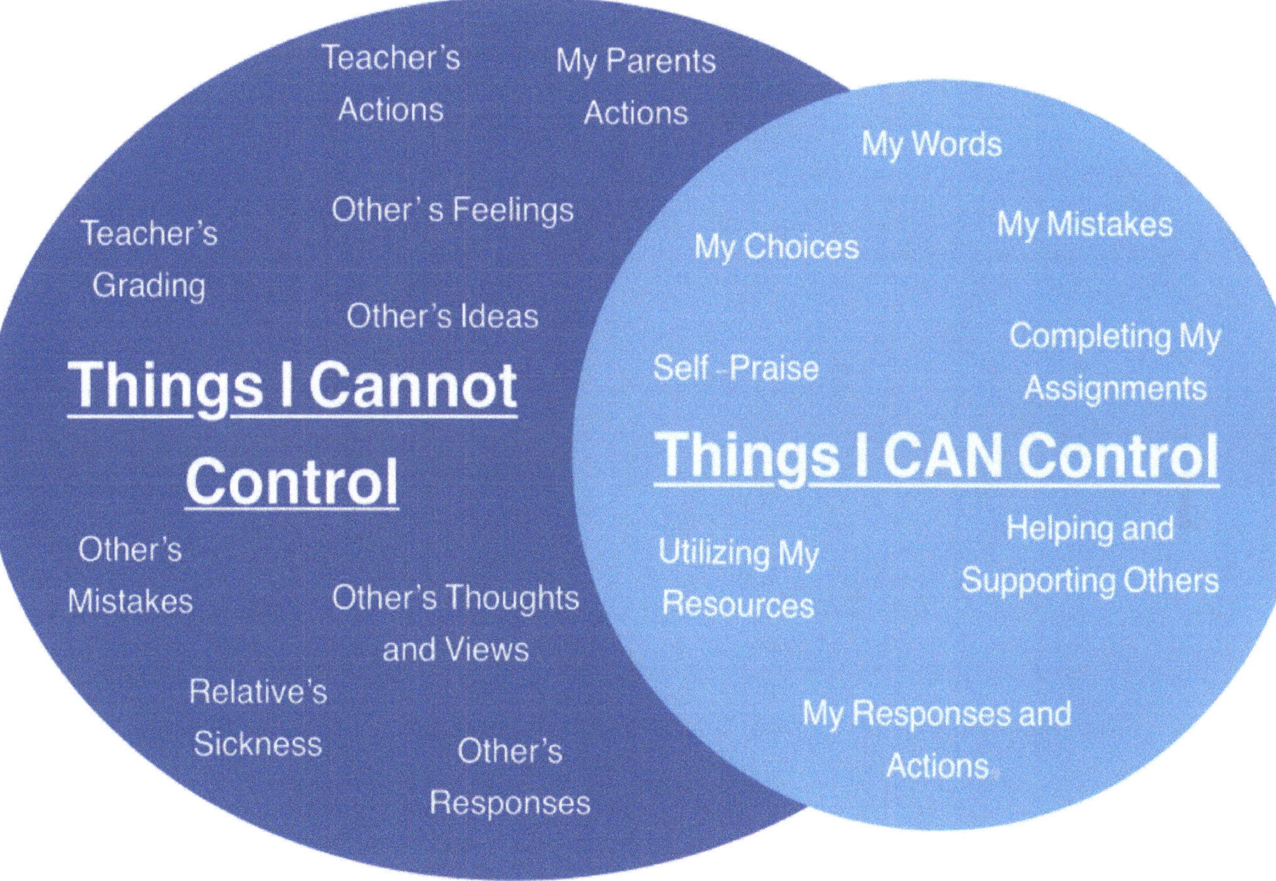

Contributors: Aisha Rehema-Gist Henderson, Jennifer Rose O'Shay & Mackenzie Zdanowitz

- Zones of Regulation

https://www.socialthinking.com/Products/zones-of-regulation-curriculum

- Your Kid is Going to Be Okay

https://www.socialthinking.com/Products/zones-of-regulation-curriculum

- Self-regulation (YouTube video)

https://www.youtube.com/watch?v=H_O1brYwdSY

- Parenting tools for self-regulation

https://www.parentingforbrain.com/self-regulation-toddler-temper-tantrums/

- Middle School – PBIS Lesson: Using Self-Control

http://internet.savannah.chatham.k12.ga.us/district/AcademicAffairs/PBIS/Documents/Lessons/Middle%20school/School-Wide/Be%20Safe/Using%20Self%20Control.pdf

About the Author

Aisha Rehema-Gist Henderson is a published poet, and motivational speaker for The I Live Movement. She has dedicated her time to educating people on Suicide Awareness, and uses her poetry book, "The Voices Who Speak Out to the Silent Killer," as an educational guide to help others who may have, or know someone with suicidal thoughts. This book can be found on Amazon. You can also find more information on The I Live Movement at www.Facebook.com/voicesofsuicide and www.theilivemovement.com.

Ms. Henderson is also a Licensed Master Social Worker who has worked in several capacities with children and families. She has done this work as a Multi-systemic Therapist, Home-Based Therapist, School Social Worker, and as an Outpatient Therapist. Based on Ms. Henderson's observations, and working in those settings, she wanted to provide students with the skill set needed to regulate their emotions in the moment. She also wanted to bring these teachings to the forefront for parents and schools to utilize. By writing this book, Ms. Henderson believed that it would assist students who are struggling in school, displaying delinquent behaviors. It would help these students learn alternative ways of resolving conflict and return back to the school system with healthier, more adaptive strategies.

Ultimately, Ms. Henderson likes to dedicate her time to collaborating with parents, teachers, School Social Workers/Counselors, and principals. This way she could help students in regulating their emotions in the classroom, with the assistance of staff and families. Ms. Henderson hopes by using the PSR technique, in both a mainstream or alternative school environment, it will encourage student success for students who are struggling.

You can reach Ms. Henderson at hende215@gmail.com if you are interested in implementing this technique in your school or have any questions.